Speed Metal

T0061532

Neo-Classical Styles
from Paganini, Bach to Rock

by Dave Celentano

Cover art - Kevin Davidson
back: l to r , Bach, Paganini, Korsakov, Vivaldi
front: Dave Celentano

To access audio visit:
www.halleonard.com/mylibrary

Enter Code
3759-0595-2959-6532

Thanks go to Mom and Dad for the support
and G.I.T. for the learning experience.

-Contents-

Track List

1. Instrumental, Indian War Song
2. Introduction/Tuning
3. <u>Example 1</u> - Slow, Jesu, Joy of Man's Desiring
4.   Fast, Jesu, Joy of Man's Desiring
5. <u>Example 2</u> - Slow, Partita Number One
6.   Fast, Partita Number One
7. <u>Example 3</u> - Slow, Melodic Exercise
8.   Fast, Melodic Exercise
9. <u>Example 4</u> - Slow, Toccata Number Four
10.   Fast, Toccata Number Four
11. <u>Example 5</u> - Slow, Etude
12.   Fast, Etude
13. <u>Example 6</u> - Slow, Caprice Number Twenty Four
14.   Fast, Caprice Number Twenty Four
15. <u>Example 7</u> - Slow, Variation Number One
16.   Fast, Variation Number One
17. <u>Example 8</u> - Slow, Variation Number Two
18.   Fast, Variation Number Two
19. <u>Example 9</u> - Slow, Variation Number Three
20.   Fast, Variation Number Three
21. <u>Example 10</u> - Slow, Variation Number Four
22.   Fast, Variation Number Four
23. <u>Example 11</u> - Slow, Variation Number Five
24.   Fast, Variation Number Five
25. <u>Example 12</u> - Slow, Variation Number Seven
26.   Fast, Variation Number Seven
27. <u>Example 13</u> - Slow, Variation Number Nine
28.   Fast, Variation Number Nine
29. <u>Example 14</u> - Slow, Variation Number Ten
30.   Fast, Variation Number Ten
31. <u>Example 15</u> - Variation Number Eleven
32. <u>Example 16</u> - Slow, The Four Seasons
33.   Fast, The Four Seasons
34. <u>Example 17</u> - Slow, The Flight of the Bumble Bee
35.   Fast, The Flight of the Bumble Bee
36. <u>Example 18</u> - Slow, Canon
37.   Fast, Canon
38. <u>Example 19</u> - Toccata
39. <u>Example 20</u> - Slow, "Fugue" from Toccata
40.   Fast, "Fugue" from Toccata
41. Instrumental, Space Walk

Ed Ouellette

Bio

Dave graduated from G.I.T. (Guitar Institute of Technology, Hollywood, California) in 1986. Since then he's written thirteen guitar instruction books for Centerstream Publications, performed on seven Starlicks instructional videos, transcribed numerous guitar tablature books for Hal Leonard Publications, performed over fifty clinics for D'Angelico strings and WRC electric guitars (Wayne R. Charvel), conducted several two hand tapping clinics at G.I.T and received a recording contract for his band 'Sir Real' in Japan.

Currently, Dave is recording a new CD with Sir Real and instructing guitar in the Los Angeles area at Grayson's Tunetown in Montrose, Dr. Music in Pasadena and Pasadena City College.

Acknowledgments

Thanks to Grayson's Tunetown, Dr. Music, Frank Green at D'Angelico strings, Jim Sullivan and Devin Thomas at Southwest Sound, Steve Whitaker (for the guitar and amp), Phil Bres (for the 'Greeny' CD), all my students, my wife Kris, and Mom & Dad.

Jesu, Joy of Man's Desiring

One of Bach's more popular pieces, this is a great little exercise to warm up with. Since it is played mostly in the twelfth fret position, there will be very minimal hand movement. Alternate picking (down, up down, up) will be the most effective way of playing this melodic piece.

by J.S. Bach

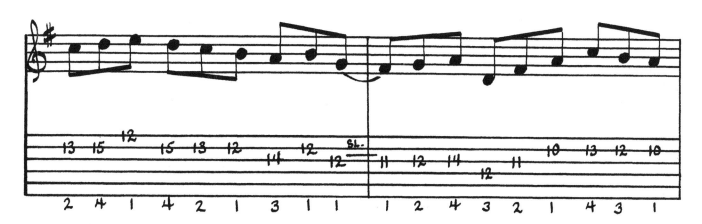

Partita Number One

This example is a little tougher than the previous and employs the harmonic minor scale (natural minor scale with a raised seventh degree) in bars 4, 6, 7, and 8. We'll also explore a little bit of sweep picking. Sweep picking is a series of down strokes or up strokes going across adjacent strings.

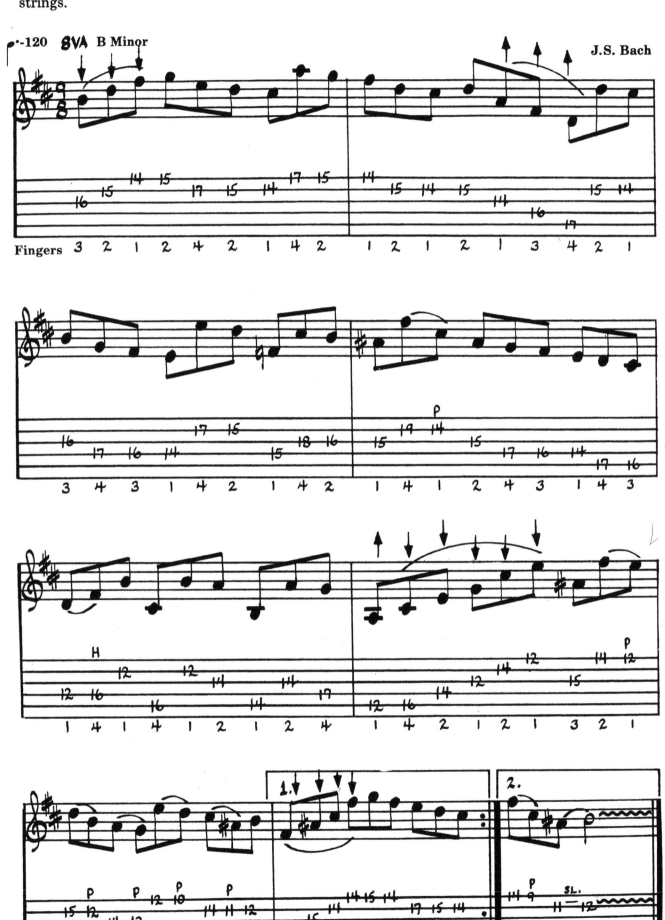

Melodic Exercise

I wrote and designed this exercise to practice sweep picking, alternate picking, string skips, hammer-ons and pull-offs. The chord progression is moving in the cycle of fourths. In other words, each chord is based four degrees above the preceding chord. This is a very typical chord sequence in classical music.

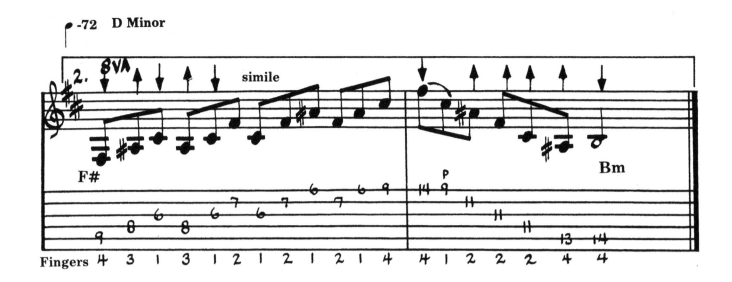

Toccata Number Four

Two new techniques worth investigating are the pedal tone usage in the first bar and the common idea of exercising the arpeggio, scale, arpeggio, scale approach in the last half of the piece. A pedal tone is a note or notes that recurs often while the melody changes above or below it.

I modified the ending a bit to make it resolve nicely on the D minor chord, because the original version kept going.

by J.S. Bach

11

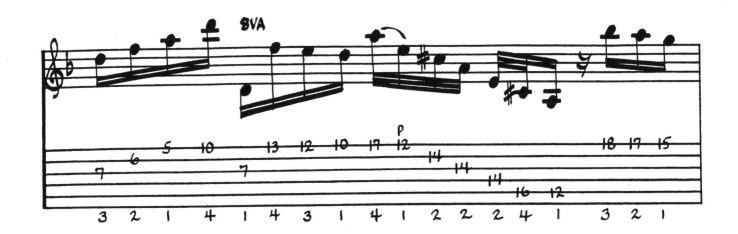

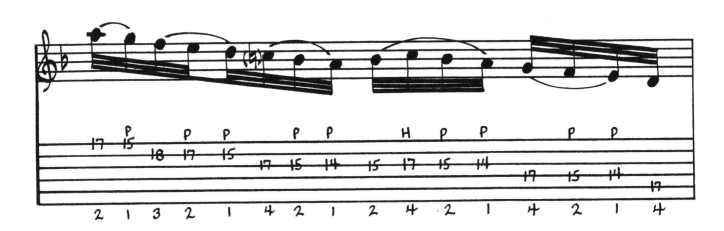

Etude

Here's a long exercise displaying many sequences. This exercise takes your fingers up and down the fretboard exposing you to the many different types of sequences. Guitar great Eddie Van Halen borrowed the first bar of this exercise in his solo "Eruption".

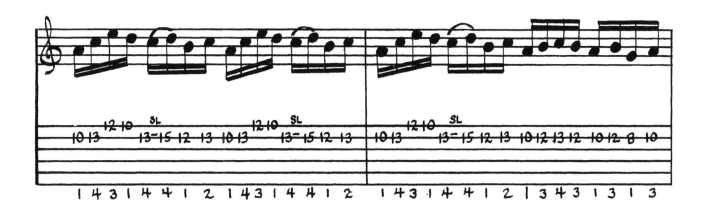

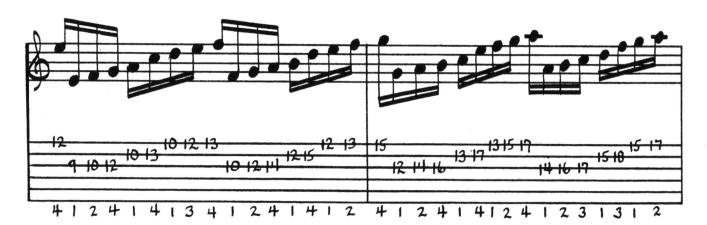

2 1 2 3 4 2 4 3 2 1 2 3 4 2 4 3   2 1 2 4 1 2 4 1 4 1 2 3 4 1 2 4

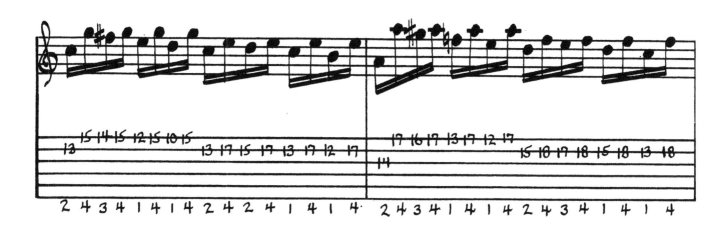

2 4 3 4 1 4 1 4 2 4 2 4 1 4 1 4   2 4 3 4 1 4 1 4 2 4 3 4 1 4 1 4

2 4 3 4 1 4 1 4 2 4 3 4 1 4 1 4   2 1 2 4 1 1 3 4 1 4 1 2 1 1 3 1

3 3 2 2 1 1 2 2 1 4 1 2 1 1 3 1   3 3 2 2 1 1 2 2 1 4 1 2 1 1 3 1   3 2 1 3 3 3 1 4 2

(Main Theme)
Caprice Number Twenty Four

In the 24th Caprice there are eleven variations. I chose the ones that are best adapted for the electric guitar. Each one develops a different technique worthy of exploring, including sweeping arpeggios, vibrato, string skipping, legato sequences and two hand tapping.

The main theme is played very majestically and establishes the chord progression incorporated in the following variations on the caprice.

by N. Paganini

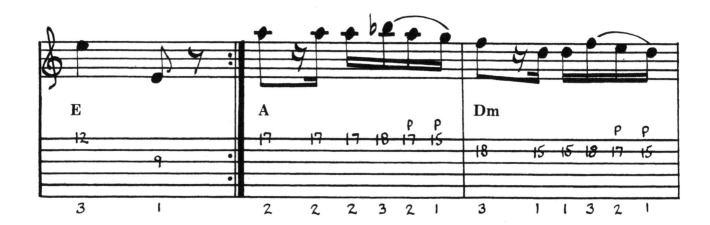

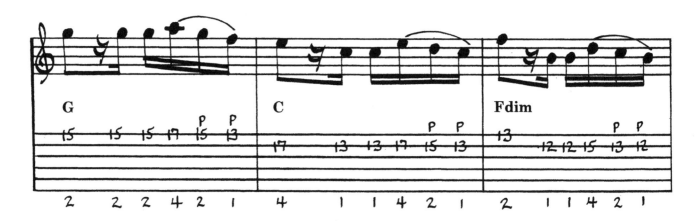

Variation Number One

Each of the sweeping arpeggios in this first variation commence with two very swift notes called **"ghost notes"**. They are to be played in the same time value of the first eighth note. The fluid sounding texture conveyed here can be achieved by working the sweeping up strokes and down strokes mega slow, until smoothness is achieved.

Variation Number Two

In this example we find a very slick and seamless flurry of notes, accomplished by using massive amounts of hammer-ons and pull-offs. This is great for building strength in the fourth finger.

♩-126 **8VA** A Minor

by N. Paganini

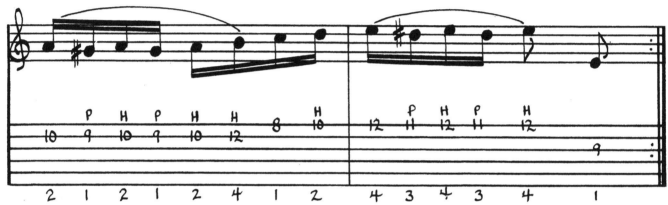

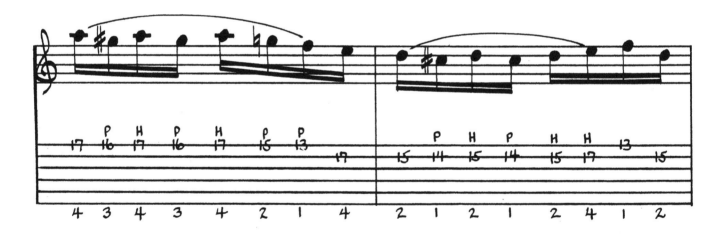

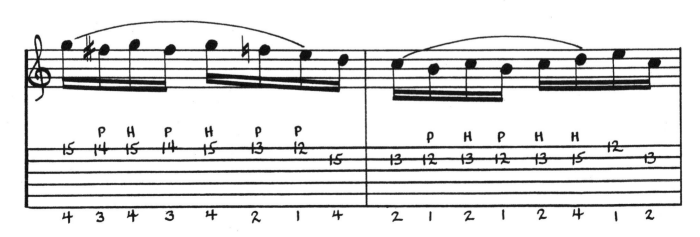

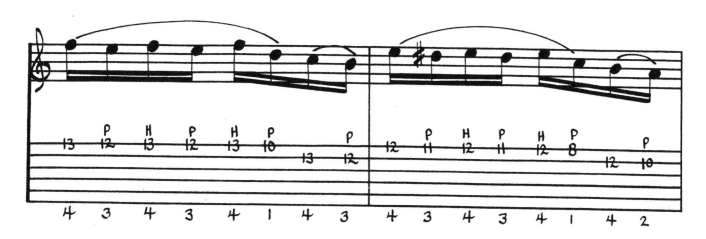

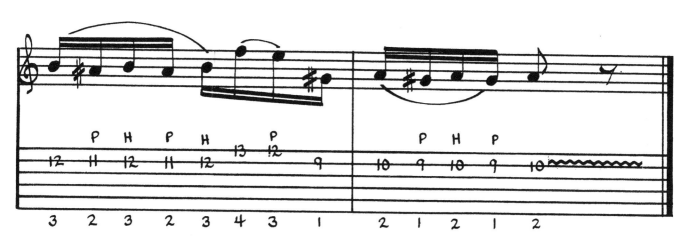

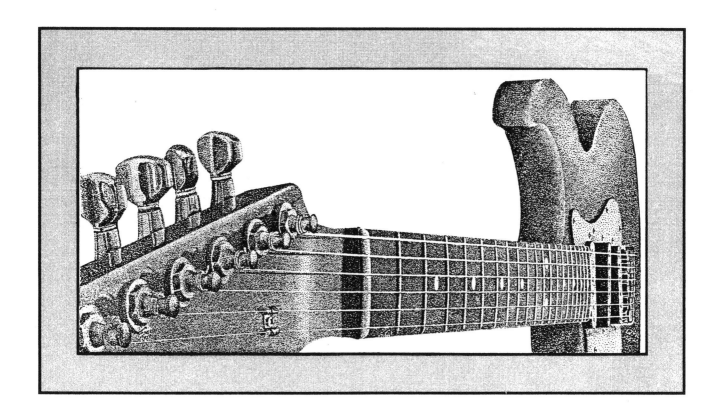

Variation Number Three

Vibrato is probably one of the least practiced techniques for rock guitarists. Since the third variation has so few notes, I thought it would do good justice to apply vibrato to all the notes.

by N. Paganini

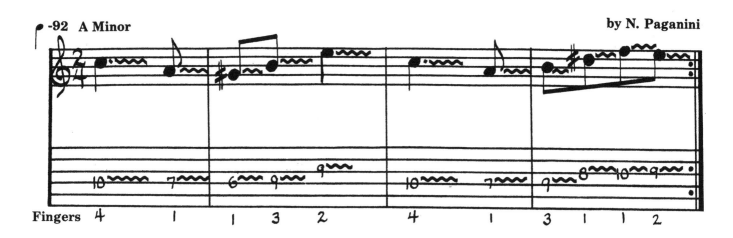

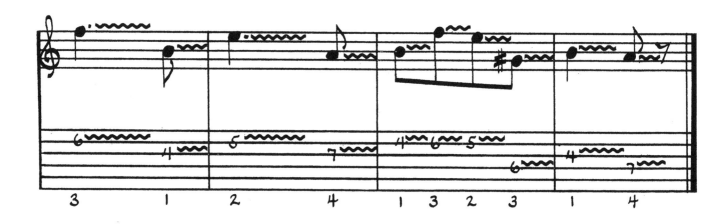

Variation Number Four

Here's a tasty way of using the chromatic scale against the chords recited in the Main Theme. All of the notes are to be played using alternate picking, with the exception of the last bar, which is sweeped with a series of up strokes.

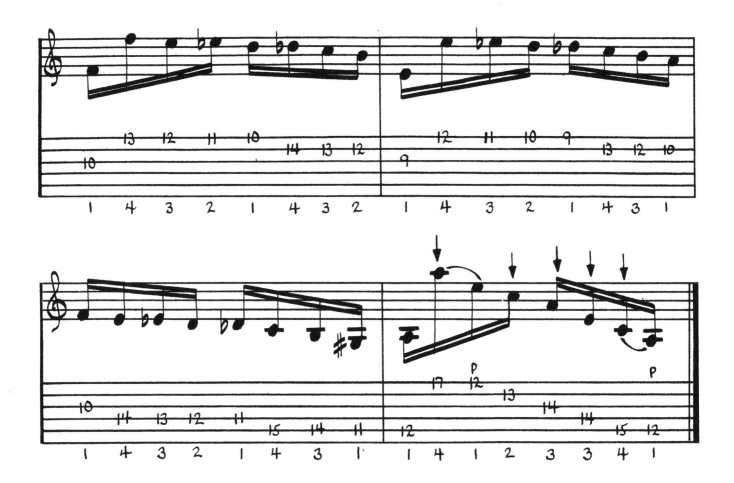

H.M. Series Strat

Variation Number Five

This variation reveals a good deal of string skipping. Finger dexterity is a must since the notes are briskly ping-ponging all over the fretboard.

Variation Number Seven

Utilizing small trills to produce a fluttering succession of notes, this exercise demands prowess and clearity in order to be executed properly.

Remember, these exercises are designed to improve and enhance your playing, so work them out slowly and carefully before shifting into fifth gear.

♩-84 A Minor

by N. Paganini

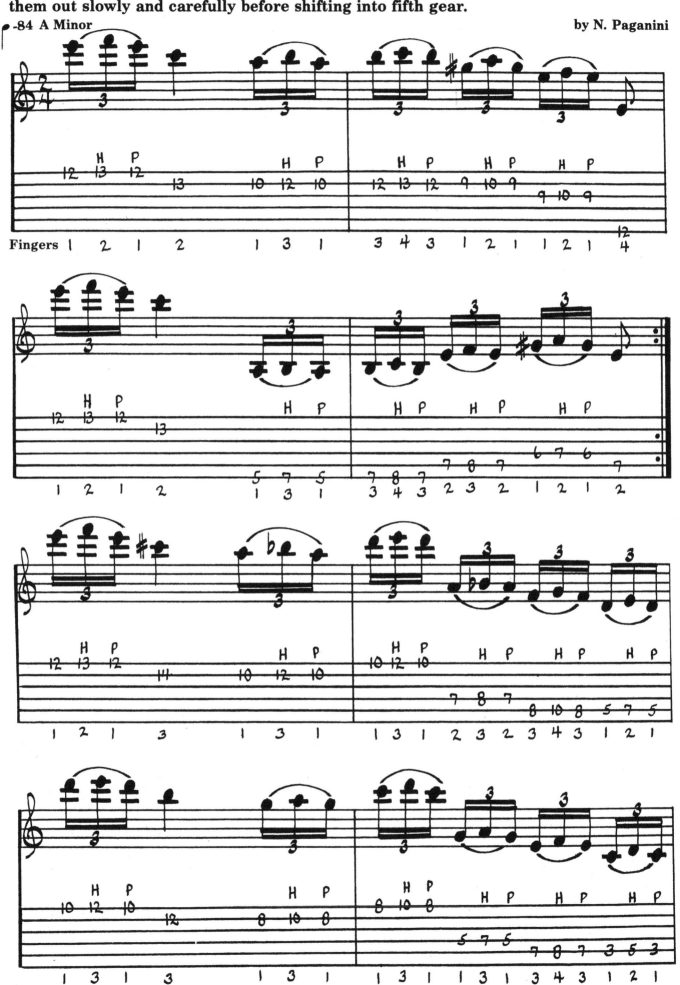

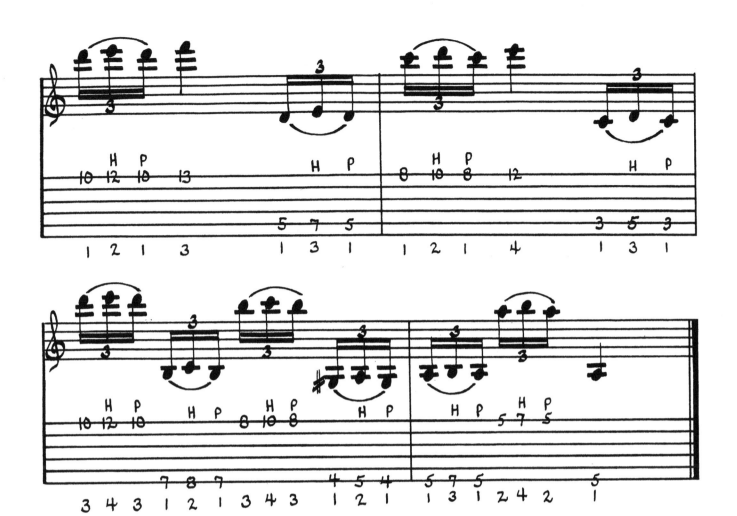

Variation Number Nine

After experimenting with many different ways of playing this piece, I discovered that two hand tapping would be excellent. Throughout the whole variation I've included all four fingers of the right hand. This allows for less hand movement, which in turn means a smoother and faster technique.

♩-96 A Minor

by N. Paganini

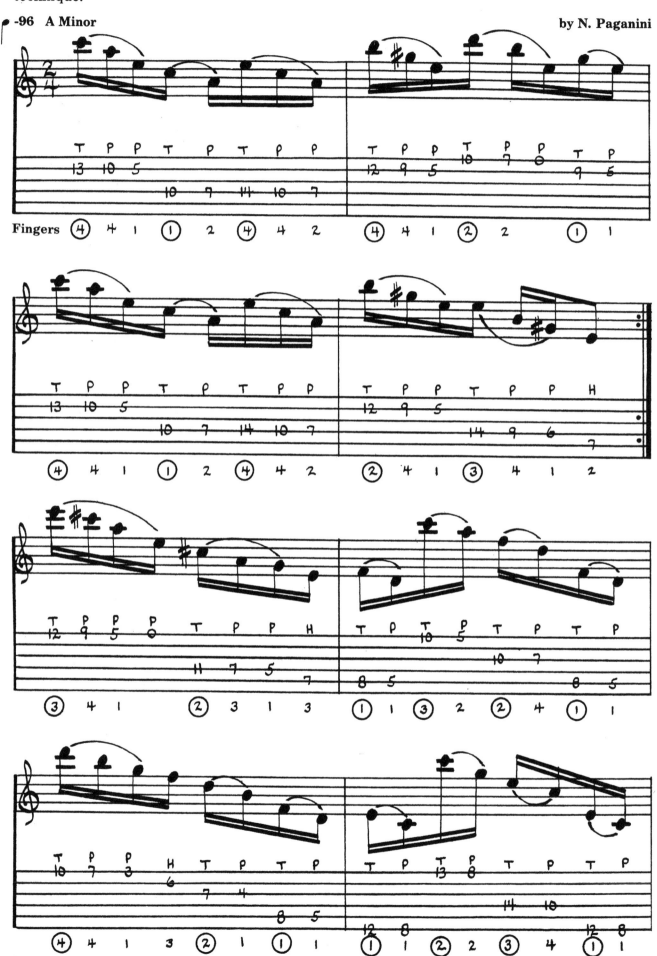

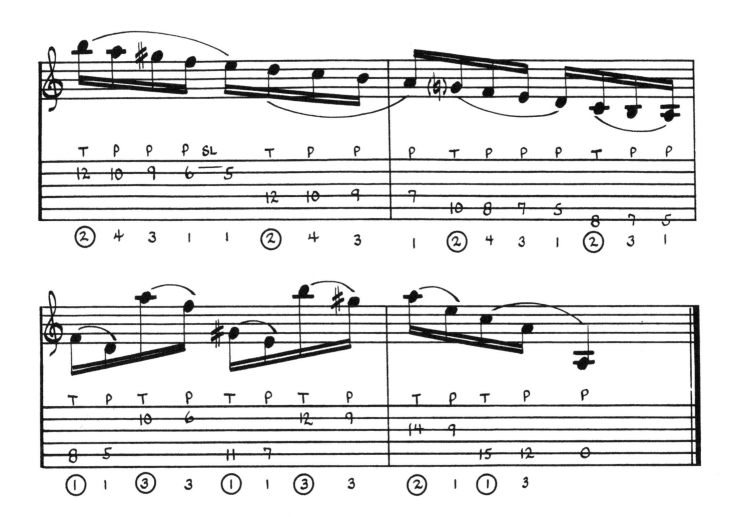

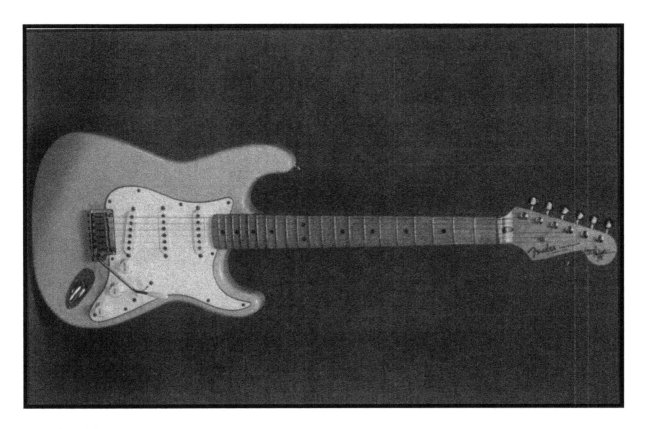

Yngwie Malmsteen
Signature Model Strat

Variation Number Ten

When a melody line includes more than just the notes of the chord, the subsequent notes are called passing tones. These are notes found in the scale, but not in the chord. This tenth variation is a great illustration of this concept.

Variation Number Eleven

Of all the variations presented here, the eleventh is by far the most radical. It jumps from huge interval skips to monstrous arpeggios blanketing most of the fretboard. Again the sweep picking technique is used to play the arpeggios.

by N. Paganini

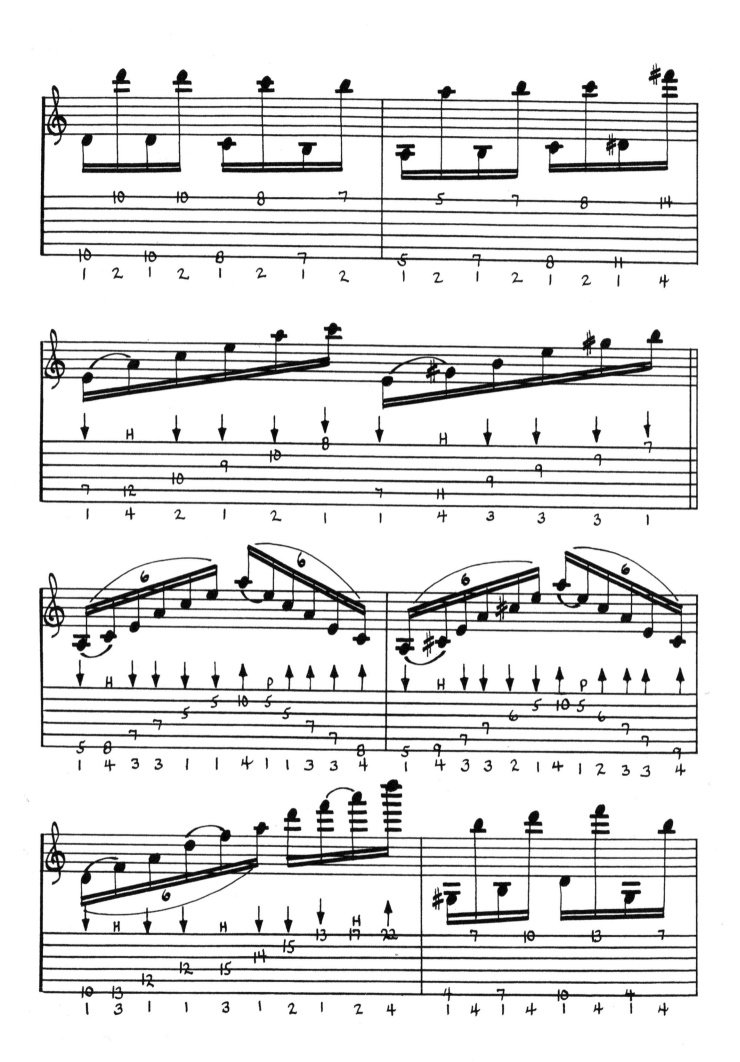

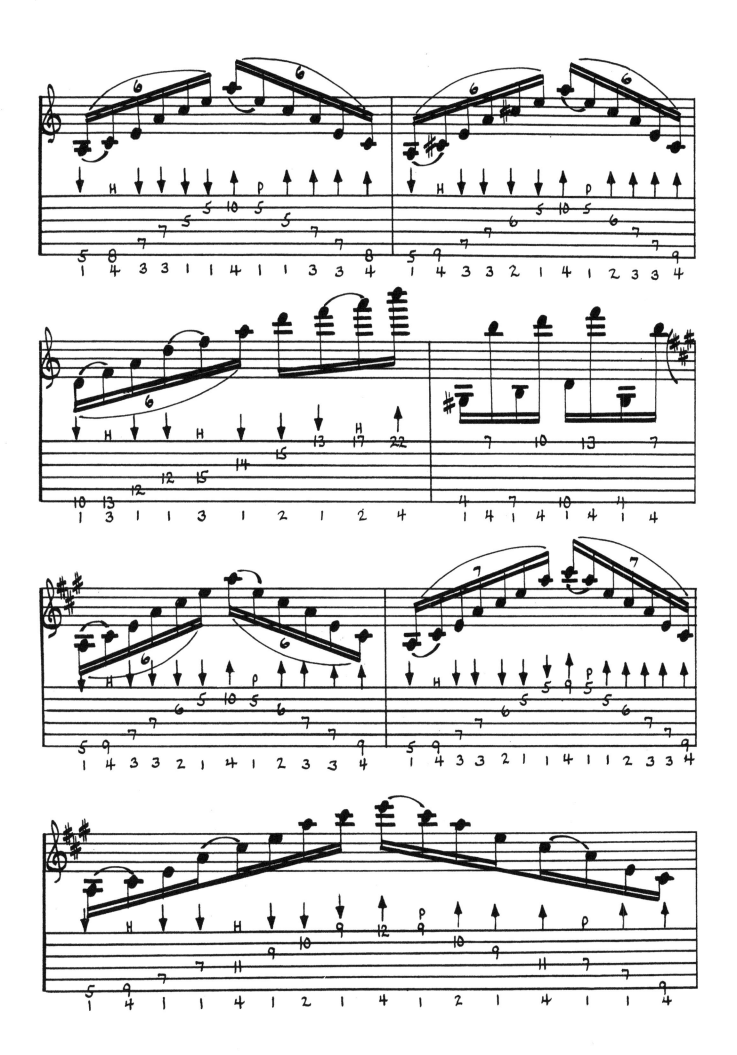

31.

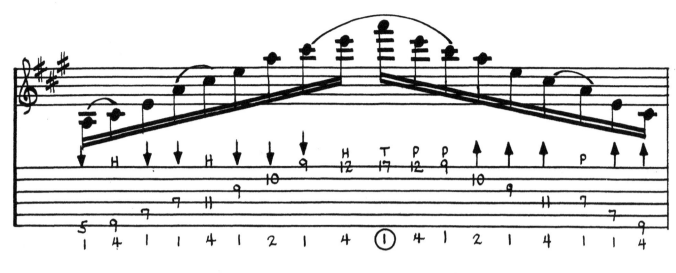

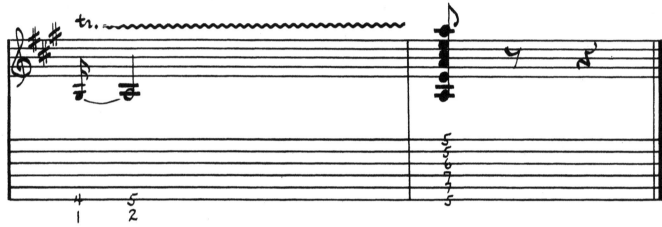

The Four Seasons

A lot of great melodies can be derived from just one string. This excerpt from Vivaldi's **The Four Seasons - Spring** is easily adapted to the B string on the guitar. This tapping idea introduces the melody in the first two bars and takes it ascending up the scale on the second string. After reaching it's peak, it creates a cascading effect finally resolving on the notes of a C major chord.

*NOTE-To play the second to the last note of this piece, you must fret your right hand **behind** your left hand and pull-off from left hand to right hand.

34

The Flight Of The Bumble Bee

Seeing that this composition is purely chromatic, I didn't dictate a particular key. When this piece is really cooking it sounds just like a bumble bee buzzing around.

by N. Rimsky-Korsakoff

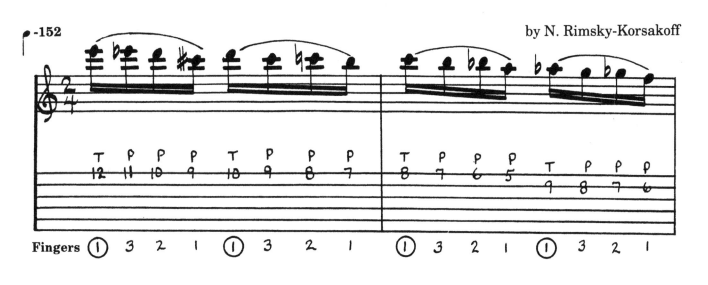

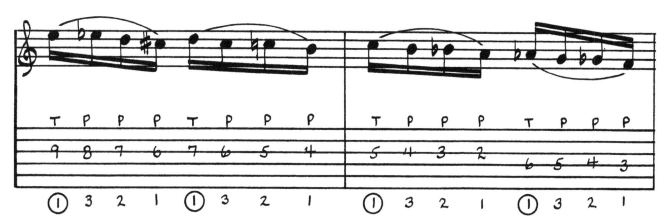

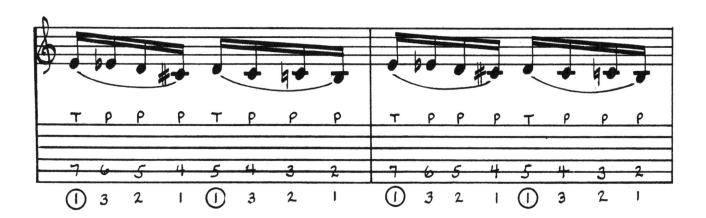

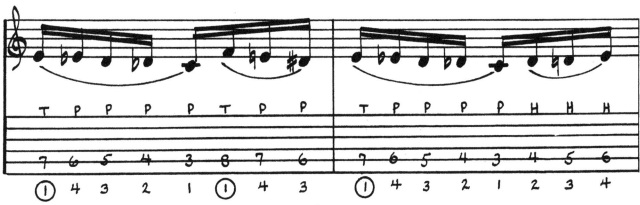

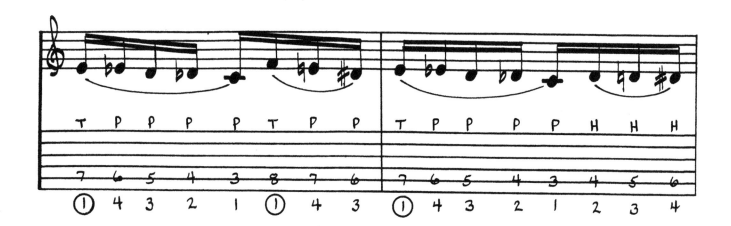

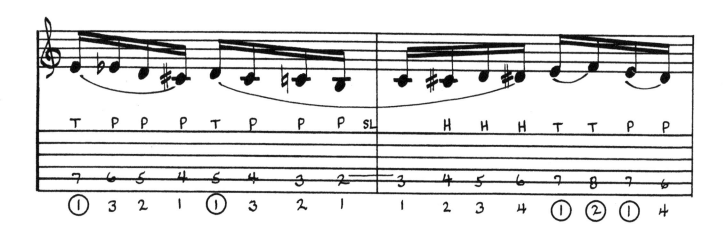

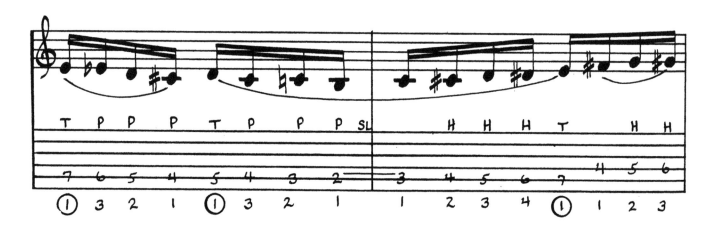

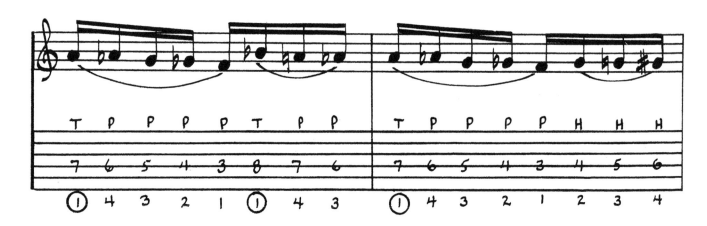

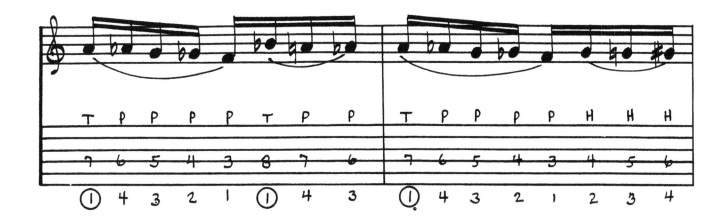

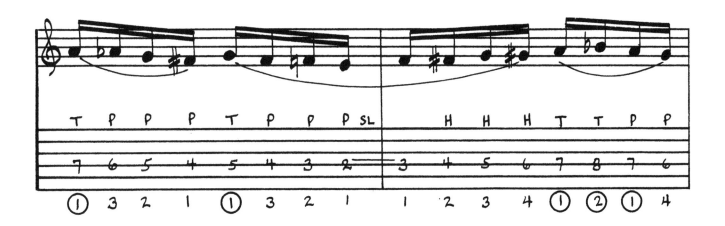

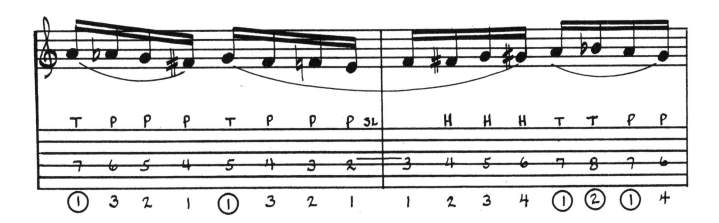

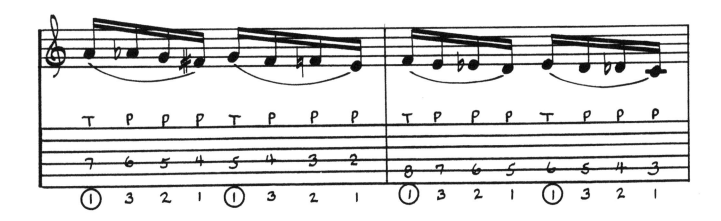

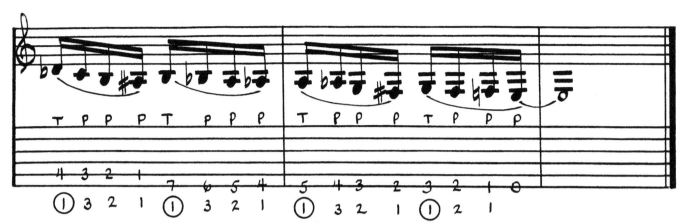

1952 Strat

Based On J. Pachelbel's "Canon"

The most important point out here is that you'll want to hold the pick between the thumb and second finger of the right hand, freeing the first finger to tap notes on the fretboard. Also, when sweep picking across the arpeggios, pick the notes over the fretboard. Example: Play the first arpeggio with the pick over or near the twenty second fret. Follow that with a tapped note on the first string, twenty second fret, with your right hand index finger. This will confine the right hand to the same area of the neck for the tapping and picking. Although this may feel awkward, after mastering the technique you'll be able to play the exercise and others like it faster.

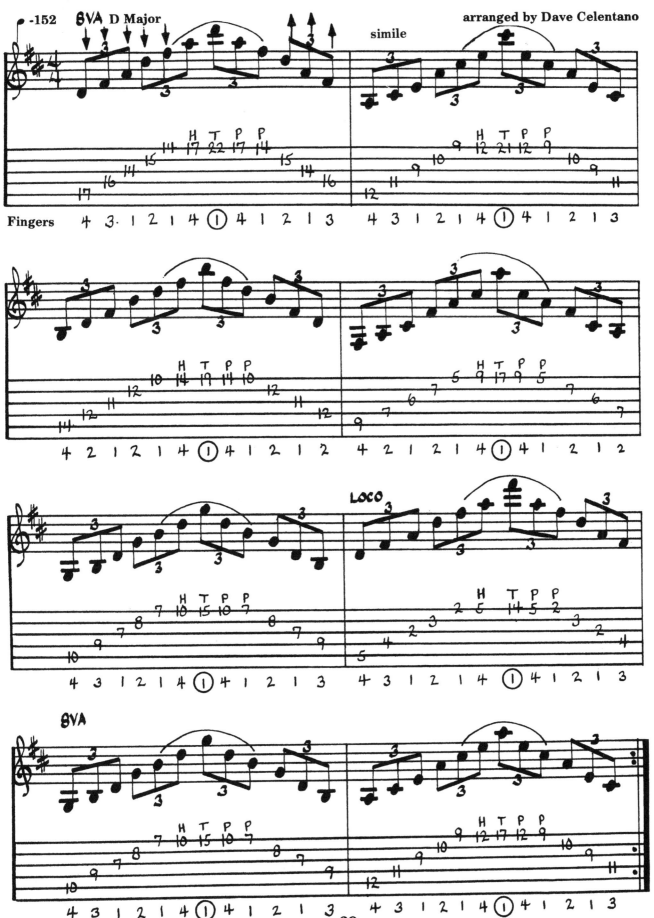

arranged by Dave Celentano

39

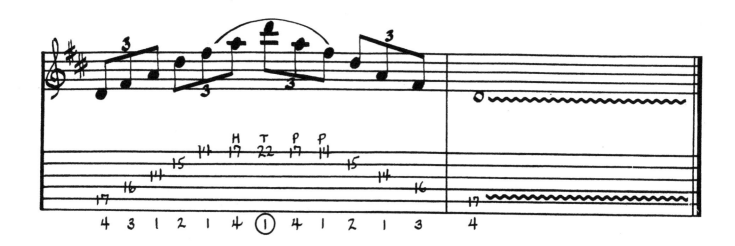

1962 Strat

Toccata

This is by far Bach's most popular piece. It was written when he was around twenty-one years old. Featuring a variety of hot phrases and sequences, this one deals primarily with two-hand tapping. The first passage of tapping uses just the second finger of the right hand, while the second passage utilizes all four fingers, creating a pedal-tone effect with the melody moving above the pedal tone. This toccata is played freely. Since each part has a different tempo, I didn't put a metronome setting. Listen to the tape accompaniment with this book to get a feeling for the tempos.

by J.S. Bach

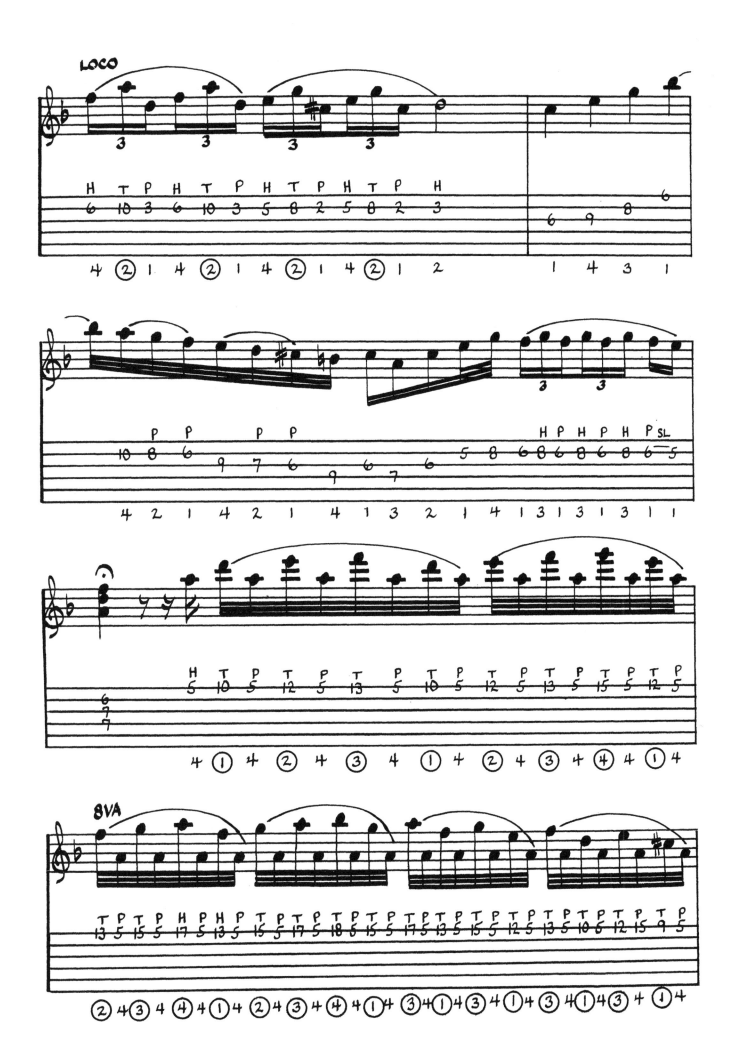

43

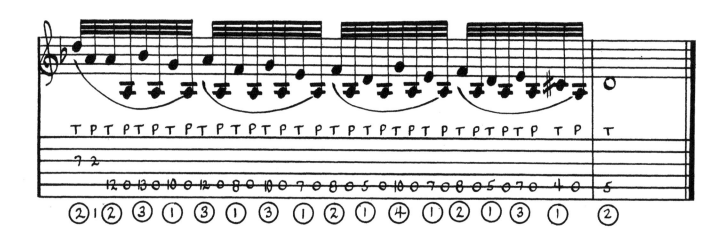

"Fugue" from Toccata

Here, we'll find the Fugue exploring a slightly different way of tapping. Like the previous example, this one also has the pedal tone affect. Only this time the melody is moving below the pedal tone.

by J.S.Bach

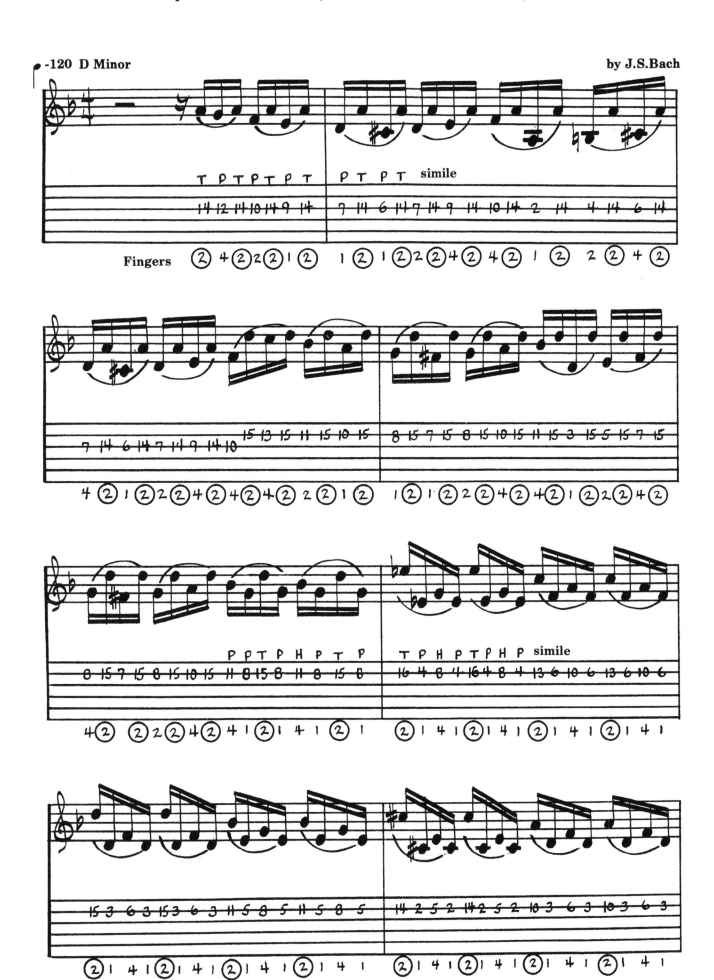

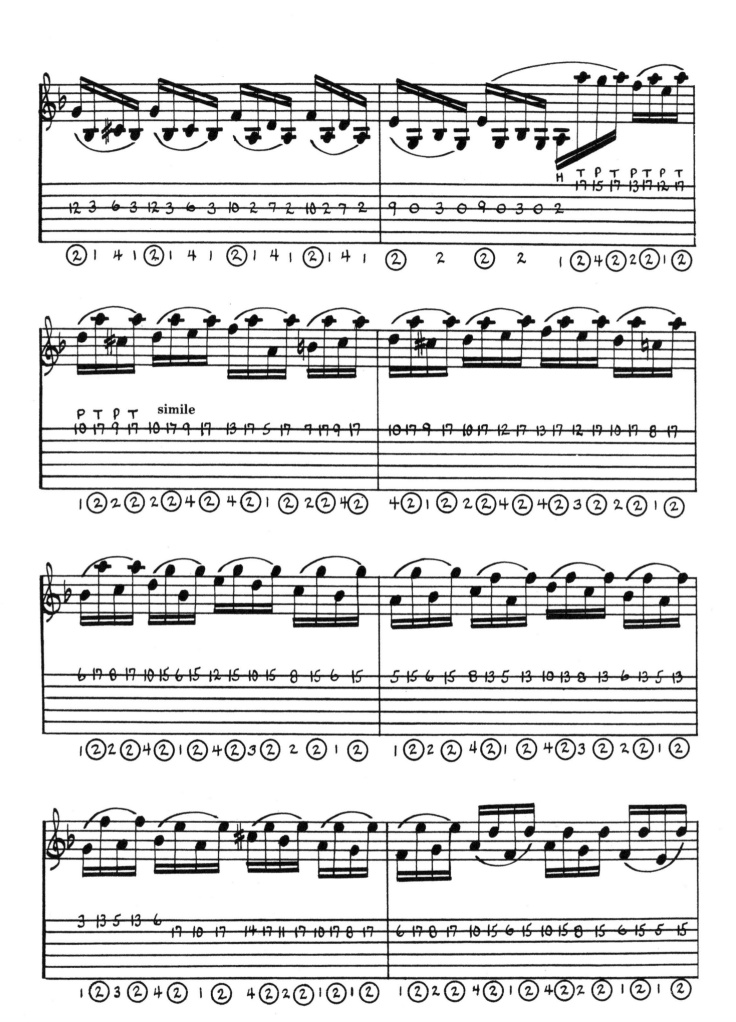

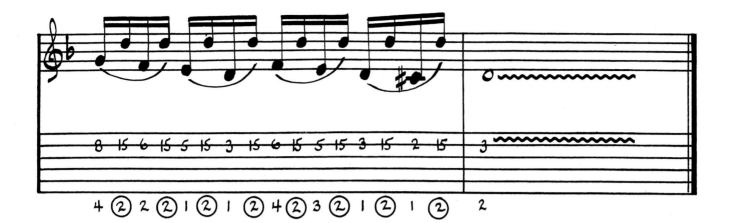

Composers in this book

Johann Pachelbel (1653-1706), a German organist and composer of suites for harpsichord and chorale preludes in fughetta (short fugue) style for organ. In 1677 he was organist at the court at Eisenach where he became a friend of J. S. Bach's father. He also wrote several motets, arias, concertos and cantatas.

Antonio Vivaldi (1675-1741), an Italian composer and violinist. He was an ordained priest, traveled extensively and was one of the most prolific composers of his time. His surviving works include concertos for a wide variety of solo instruments with orchestra (he was one of the first composers to use clarinets), chamber music, secular cantatas, church music and oratorio and operas. Despite his tremendous output he was by no means a conventional composer, and much of his instrumental work shows a lively and fertile imagination. Bach admired him, and transcribed some of his concertos.

Johann Sebastian Bach (1685-1750), the chief influences in Bachs music are the Lutheran chorale, the church and organ music of his predecessors and the contemporary French and Italian styles in instrumental music. In his lifetime he had a great reputation as a organist, but his music was considered by many to be over-elaborate and old-fashioned. His music was written for a practical purpose - for the court orchestra, for Sunday service, for instruction of his sons, for gratification of patrons and for his own use. Bach was a universal musician, a musical genius, whose music has a universal appeal. It is steeped in the flavor of its period, yet belongs to all time.

Niccolo Paganini (1782-1840), an Italian violinist and composer, one of the most famous in musical history. He also played guitar and viola. The extraordinary range of his technical mastery can be found in his 24 caprices for solo violin. He also wrote violin concertos and chamber music for guitar and strings. Tall and skeletal, he played the violin with such verve and demonic intensity that many people believed him to be inspired by the Devil.

Nikolay Andreyevich Rimsky-Korsakov (1844-1908), a Russian composer, and member of Balakirev's circle known as 'The Mighty Handful' due to his strong influence of national ideas in his early work. His clear and brilliant orchestrations had a marked effect on Stravinsky. He gave his main creative efforts to the composition of operas, which are his greatest achievement.

More Great Guitar Books from Centerstream...

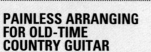

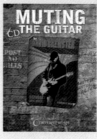